THE CHINESE HOROSCOPES LIBRARY

PIG

KWOK MAN-HO

DK

A DORLING KINDERSLEY BOOK

Senior Editor — Sharon Lucas
Art Editor — Camilla Fox
Managing Editor — Krystyna Mayer
Managing Art Editor — Derek Coombes
DTP Designer — Doug Miller
Production Controller — Antony Heller
US Editor — Laaren Brown

Artworks: Danuta Mayer 4, 8, 11, 17, 27, 29, 31, 33, 35;
Giuliano Fornari 21; Jane Thomson; Sarah Ponder.

Special Photography by Steve Gorton. Thank you to the Bristol City Museum & Art Gallery,
Oriental Section; The British Museum, Chinese Post Office, The Powell-Cotton Museum,
and The Board of Trustees of the Victoria & Albert Museum.

Additional Photography: Peter Chadwick, Eric Crichton, Michael Crockett, Geoff Dann,
Jo Foord, Steve Gorton, Dave King, Clive Streeter.

Picture Credits: Bridgeman Art Library/Oriental Museum, Durham University 15; Circa
Photo Library 13, 19bl; Courtesy of The Board of Trustees of the Victoria & Albert
Museum 22cr.

First American Edition, 1994
4 6 8 10 9 7 5

Published in the United States by DK Publishing, Inc., 95 Madison Avenue,
New York, New York 10016

Copyright © 1994
Dorling Kindersley Limited, London
Text copyright © 1994 ICOREC

**Visit us on the World Wide Web at
http://www.dk.com**

ISBN 1-56458-605-7
Library of Congress Catalog Number 93-48006

Reproduced by GRB Editrice, Verona, Italy
Printed and bound in Hong Kong by Imago

CONTENTS

INTRODUCING CHINESE HOROSCOPES

For thousands of years, the Chinese have used their astrology and religion to establish a harmony between people and the world around them.

The exact origins of the twelve animals of Chinese astrology – the Rat, Ox, Tiger, Rabbit, Dragon, Snake, Horse, Ram, Monkey, Rooster, Dog, and Pig – remain a mystery. Nevertheless, these animals are important in Chinese astrology. They are much more than general signposts to the year and to the possible good or bad times ahead for us all. The twelve animals of Chinese astrology are considered to be a reflection of the Universe itself.

YIN AND YANG

The many differences in our natures, moods, health, and fortunes reflect the wider changes within the Universe. The Chinese believe that every single thing in the Universe is held in balance by the dynamic, cosmic forces of yin and yang. Yin is feminine, watery, and cool; the force of the Moon and the rain. Yang is masculine, solid, and hot; the force of the Sun and the Earth. According to ancient Chinese belief, the concentrated essences of yin and yang became the four seasons, and the scattered essences of yin and yang became the myriad creatures that are found on Earth.

YIN AND YANG SYMBOL
White represents the female force of yin, and black represents the masculine force of yang.

The twelve animals of Chinese astrology are all associated with either yin or yang. The forces of yin rise as Winter approaches. These forces decline with the warmth of Spring, when yang begins to assert itself. Even in the course of a normal day, yin and yang are at work, constantly changing and balancing. These forces also naturally rise and fall within us all.

Everyone has their own internal balance of yin and yang. This affects our tempers, ambitions, and health. We also respond to the changes of weather, to the environment, and to the people who surround us.

THE FIVE ELEMENTS

All that we can touch, taste, or see is divided into five basic types or elements – wood, fire, earth, gold, and water. Everything in the Universe can be linked to one of these elements.

For example, the element water is linked to the Rat and to the Pig. This element is also linked to the color black, salty-tasting food, the season of Winter, and the emotion of fear. The activity of these various elements indicates the fortune that may befall us.

AN INDIVIDUAL DISCOVERY

Chinese astrology can help you balance your yin and yang. It can also tell you which element you are, and the colors, tastes, parts of the body, or emotions that are linked to your particular sign. Your fortune can be prophesied according to the year, month, day, and hour in which you were born. You can identify the type of people to whom you are attracted, and the career that will suit your character. You can understand your changes of mood, your reactions to other places and to other people. In essence, you can start to discover what makes you an individual.

DIVINATION STICKS
Another ancient and popular method of Chinese fortune-telling is using special divination sticks to obtain a specific reading from prediction books.

CASTING YOUR HOROSCOPE

*The Chinese calendar is based on the movement of the
Moon, unlike the calendar used in the Western world,
which is based on the movement of the Sun.*

Before you begin to cast your
Chinese horoscope, check your year
of birth on the chart on pages 44 to
45. Check particularly carefully if
you were born in the early months of
the year. The Chinese year does not
usually begin until January or
February, and you might belong to the
previous Chinese year. For
example, if you were born in 1961
you might assume that you were
born in the Year of the Ox.
However, if your birthday falls
before February 15 you belong to the
previous Chinese year, which is the
Year of the Rat.

THE SIXTY-YEAR CYCLE

The Chinese measure the passing of
time by cycles of sixty years. The
twelve astrological animals appear
five times during the sixty-year
cycle, and they appear in a slightly
different form every time. For
example, if you were born in 1947

you are a Pig Passing the Mountain,
but if you were born in 1971, you
are a Pig in the Garden.

MONTHS, DAYS, AND HOURS

The twelve lunar months of the
Chinese calendar do not correspond
exactly with the twelve Western
calendar months. This is because
Chinese months are lunar, whereas
Western months are solar. Chinese
months are normally twenty-nine to
thirty days long, and every three to
four years an extra month is added to
keep approximately in step with the
Western year.

One Chinese hour is equal to two
Western hours, and the twelve
Chinese hours correspond to the
twelve animal signs.

The year, month, day, and hour
of birth are the keys to Chinese
astrology. Once you know them,
you can start to unlock your personal
Chinese horoscope.

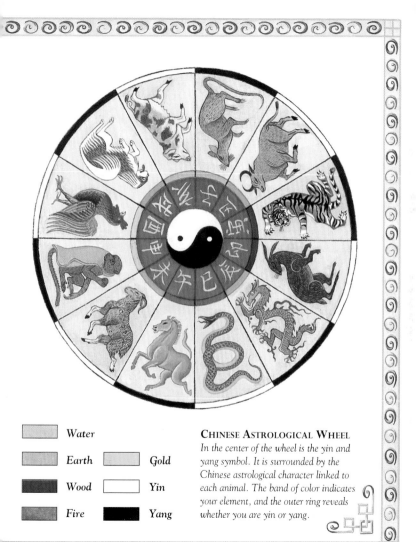

	Water
	Earth
	Wood
	Fire

	Gold
	Yin
	Yang

CHINESE ASTROLOGICAL WHEEL

In the center of the wheel is the yin and yang symbol. It is surrounded by the Chinese astrological character linked to each animal. The band of color indicates your element, and the outer ring reveals whether you are yin or yang.

MYTHS AND LEGENDS

The Jade Emperor, heaven's ruler, asked to see the Earth's twelve
most interesting animals. When they arrived, he was impressed
by the Pig's peacefulness, and awarded it twelfth place.

Although the Jade Emperor named the Pig the twelfth and last animal in the Chinese zodiac, the pig is nevertheless a powerful figure in Chinese belief, and is a revered symbol of virility.

In China the pig is usually black or white, and very rarely pink. Chinese Muslims do not eat pork, and pork is never offered to the Chinese god Xuan-tan because he is believed to be a Muslim. Young women avoid eating knuckle of pork because it has strong associations with pregnancy.

However, pregnant women are actively encouraged to eat this dish because it is considered to be extremely nourishing for both mother and unborn child.

SLEEPING PIG
This Chinese sleeping pig is pinkish stoneware, with a delicate olive-brown glaze. It is an artifact from the T'ang dynasty (618–906).

THE ADVENTURES OF PIGSY

The most famous pig in Chinese legend is Pigsy, a greedy bully and coward. Pigsy was a member of the strange band of pilgrims who accompanied the monk Hsuan Chuang on his journey to India to bring back the most complete set of Buddhist scriptures. Pigsy was a reincarnated god who had fallen from favor. Although he was born with divine powers, he had the body and nature of a pig. He joined a prosperous peasant family and

"SHANG" DYNASTY PIG

This pig is a copy of a Shang dynasty bronze, from a period in which many animals were cast in bronze.

worked very hard, plowing up the ground with his feet and nose. Pigsy had a voracious appetite, and although the family was fairly wealthy by peasant standards, Pigsy almost ate them out of house and home, devouring more than one hundred cakes at breakfast alone.

He became increasingly attracted to the daughter of the family and insisted that he should be allowed to marry her. When her family refused to agree, he locked the daughter in an old part of the house and would allow no one near her.

Eventually the monk Hsuan Chuang, came by, accompanied by Monkey, the reprobate. Hsuan Chuang and Monkey rescued the peasant girl, and Monkey and Pigsy fought an epic battle. Pigsy suddenly remembered the words of Kuan Yin, the goddess of mercy. Many years before, she had said that she would send him a monk, and if he served the monk, Pigsy would be reborn as a god in the next life. Pigsy concluded that Hsuan Chuang must have been sent to him by Kuan Yin.

Pigsy stopped fighting Monkey and joined him instead in the service of Hsuang Chuang. Using his strength as well as his huge appetite, Pigsy worked his passage to India, although sometimes his "pig-headed" nature got the better of him.

PERSONALITY

The Pig is a calm and tolerant creature. Although it mixes well with other people in a variety of environments, it can sometimes be reticent with strangers.

You have diverse interests and are eager to learn. Variety is much more appealing to you than intensive study in a single area. You are optimistic and prefer to see the best in people, or the bright side of a difficult situation.

MOTIVATION

You indulge in life's pleasures, and other people share your enjoyment, too. Money, competition, and ambition do not interest you, but you like to know that your financial affairs are in a good state of health. You are fortunate, and opportunities invariably appear when you need them most.

FIGHTING PIG

The coiled, fighting animals shown in this ancient Chinese bronze are a pig and a tiger.

THE INNER PIG

You are interested in the motives behind people's actions, and are usually tolerant of others unless you are absolutely forced to change your personal opinion. Aggression and arguments make you recoil. You prefer to listen to other people, and interact only when you feel at ease. However, once you are relaxed, you are talkative and chat enthusiastically about a whole range of subjects. You steer clear of extreme behavior, and always favor compromise. When making a decision, you take your time and tend to ask for your

PINK PIG
This sturdy, unglazed model of a pink pig dates from China's T'ang dynasty (7th–8th century).

friends' support and guidance. However, if you have to complete a task alone, you generally apply yourself without complaint. You have a forgiving nature and try to give others a second chance, but then you tread warily in the future. You do your best to resist potentially dangerous situations, but can withstand setbacks. Your reputation is important to you, and you guard it jealously. When you are pushed to your limits, your temper is fierce.

Once your friendships have been formed, you are devoted to your friends – always willing to overlook their faults, and sympathetic and available when they are in times of need. In emotional relationships you are loyal and optimistic, and you make a protective parent.

In all relationships, and in your life, once you have found your niche you are happy and content.

THE PIG CHILD
The young Pig is a reasonable and peaceful creature, but may waste its talents through daydreaming or carelessness. It needs a gentle guiding hand, as well as private space for personal reflection.

· PIG ·
LOVE

The Pig is affectionate, imaginative, and fascinated by love.
It is blessed with innocence and vivacity, that enable it to
experience romance to the full.

You have immense enthusiasm — you want everything immediately and are not afraid of what others may think of you. However, you are discriminating, and it may take you a long time to find a suitable life partner. Once you have found a soulmate, you should remain peaceful and optimistic.

You expect your partner to behave as honestly as you, and will feel resentful if your partner fails to share your sense of love and devotion.

Even when you are in a committed relationship, you still prefer to maintain an aura of independence. Essentially, however, you are emotionally dependent and dedicated to your relationship.

Ideally, you are suited to the Rabbit and the Ram. You share the Rabbit's honesty and serenity, but it may find you too outrageous. Like the Ram, you love beauty, but the Ram could become annoyed by your longing for immediacy. You share the Horse's vitality and honesty, but

GODDESS OF LOVE
Kuan Yin is a powerful figure in Chinese mythology. Once a male Buddhist deity, she is now known as the goddess of mercy, and as Sung-tzu, the giver of children.

CHINESE COMPATIBILITY WHEEL

Find your animal sign, then look for the animals that share its background color – the Pig has a green background and is most compatible with the Rabbit and the Ram. The symbol in the center of the wheel represents double happiness.

the Horse will have to learn to accept your independent moods. The Rat relishes your attentiveness and shares your sense of luxury, but may find itself frustrated by your apparent naïveté. The Ox will appreciate your openness, although your spendthrift tendency will cause it some distress. The Tiger shares your humor and need for personal space; the Dragon will charm you with its energy,

ORCHID

In China, the orchid, or Lan Hua, is an emblem of love and beauty. It is also a fertility symbol and represents many offspring.

individuality, and curiosity, and the protective Dog will benefit from your optimism.

The Monkey's wily tricks will not impress you, and it will find your charm disarming. You can see through the Rooster's superficiality and will calm its spirit. Another Pig could prove to be a good friend and lover, but you will have many misunderstandings. Perhaps you are too frank for the Snake, but since you are both sensual creatures, you are certainly physically compatible.

· PIG ·
CAREER

The Pig is ambitious and hardworking. It aims to achieve a comfortable lifestyle, but does not allow its ambition to override its enjoyment of life.

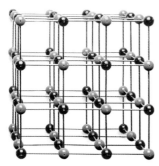

SCIENTIST
The world of science, particularly research work, appeals greatly to the Pig. This is because scientific research involves very hard work, and potentially considerable rewards. The Pig prefers to work on its own and at its own pace. It does its best to avoid competition, professional battles, and power games.

Molecular model of salt

Microscope

CHEMIST
It is important for the Pig to feel personally satisfied with the quality of its work. As a chemist, the Pig's careful diligence is used to the fullest.

Copper chloride

Copper carbonate

Typesetter's composing stick

LINCHPIN

This ancient Chinese linchpin is decorated with a pig's head. This is appropriate, because it links a practical object with the technically gifted Pig.

Linchpin

Pieces of type

TECHNICIAN

The Pig has a natural aptitude for anything technical. Although it may take some time before the Pig finds a suitable career, it is always likely to gain satisfaction from technical work, such as typesetting.

MUSICIAN

The independence of the musician's life suits the Pig well. This musical instrument is a Chin Ching, a lute originating from China's Chin dynasty (221-206BC).

Chinese lute

SKILLED WORKER

The Pig is hard-working and talented. Consequently, it is suited to a career as a skilled worker. A shoemaker's work is highly skilled, involving stitching, gluing, riveting, and nailing.

Parts of a shoe

HEALTH

Yin and yang are in a continual state of flux within the body. Good health is dependent upon the balance of yin and yang being constantly harmonious.

There is a natural minimum and maximum level of yin and yang in the human body. The body's energy is known as ch'i and is a yang force. The movement of ch'i in the human body is complemented by the movement of blood, which is a yin force. The very slightest displacement of the balance of yin or yang in the body can quickly lead to poor health.

LINGCHIH FUNGUS

The fungus shown in this detail from a Ch'ing dynasty bowl is the "immortal" lingchih fungus, which symbolizes longevity.

GINSENG

This powerful, non-toxic herb has been used medicinally in China for over two thousand years.

Yang illness can be cured by yin treatment, and yin illness can be cured by yang treatment. Everybody has their own individual balance of yin and yang. It is likely that a hot-tempered person will have strong yang forces, and that a peaceful person will have strong yin forces. Your nature is closely identified with your health, and before Chinese medicine can be prescribed, your moods have to be carefully taken into account. A balance of joy, anger, sadness, happiness, worry, pensiveness, and fear must be maintained. This fine balance is known in China as the Harmony of the Seven Sentiments.

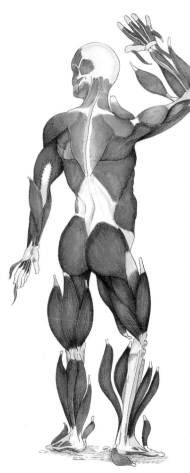

Born in the Year of the Pig, you are associated with the element water. This element is linked with the kidneys, bladder, ears, and bones. These are the parts of the body that are relevant to the pattern of your health. You are also associated with the emotion of fear and with salty-tasting food.

The herb ginseng (*Panax schinseng*) is associated with your astrological sign. Oriental ginseng is native to China and is considered to be warming and invigorating. Its yang qualities strengthen the body's resistance, and it is usually prescribed as a sedative or tonic. American ginseng was introduced into China in the 18th century and is considered to be cooling. Its yin qualities are used to quench thirst, lower fever, and ease irritability.

Chinese medicine is highly specific; therefore, never take ginseng or any other herb unless you are following professional advice from a fully qualified Chinese or Western doctor.

ASTROLOGY AND ANATOMY
Your element, water, is particularly associated with the urinary tract. The kidneys are yin organs, and the bladder is a yang organ.

· PIG ·
LEISURE

The Pig likes to go off in search of adventures on the spur of the moment. However, it enjoys life's comforts and will always choose luxury rather than simplicity.

SOCIALIZING
The consumption of food and drink in a social environment is one of the Pig's favorite pursuits. This porcelain boar's-head tureen is Chinese export ware from the 1760s.

Chinese boar's-head tureen

Globe artichoke

Chef's knives

COOKING
Preparing good food and enjoying home comforts are great sources of pleasure for the Pig, since it has epicurean tastes.

Pen and
ink

WRITING
*Reading and writing poetry and novels are often
rewarding, as well as pleasurable, pastimes for the
Pig. When a Pig takes up writing seriously, it is
likely to win literary prizes.*

Silver
trophy

CLIMBING
*Remote landscapes, the countryside, sea,
and mountains are relaxing environments
for the Pig. It finds mountain climbing and
rock climbing challenging, but
extremely energizing.*

Climbing
equipment

ADVENTURES
*Equipped with just the bare
necessities, the Pig loves to search for
adventures at a moment's notice. This
descendeur is used to control the speed
of an abseil in rock climbing.*

Climbing
protection
devices

Descendeur

SYMBOLISM

*Each astrological animal is linked with a certain food,
direction, color, emotion, association, and symbol. The Pig
is also associated with the season of Winter.*

COLOR

*In china, black is the color
of honor. It is also the
color that is linked with
the Pig. This black
stoneware pig is from
ancient China.*

Chinese stoneware pig

FOOD

*There are five tastes according to
Chinese astrology – salty, acrid,
bitter, sour, and sweet. Salty foods
are associated with the Pig.*

Grains of salt

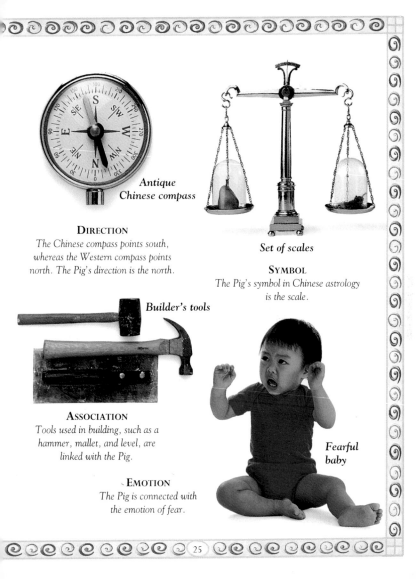

Antique Chinese compass

DIRECTION
The Chinese compass points south, whereas the Western compass points north. The Pig's direction is the north.

Set of scales

SYMBOL
The Pig's symbol in Chinese astrology is the scale.

Builder's tools

ASSOCIATION
Tools used in building, such as a hammer, mallet, and level, are linked with the Pig.

EMOTION
The Pig is connected with the emotion of fear.

Fearful baby

PIG PASSING BY

~ 1935 1995 ~

This is a classic Pig personality — although you may suffer while you are young, you should invariably enjoy happier times as you grow older.

You are associated with a bud breaking forth, symbolizing the struggle of coming out of the bud's sheath, and the glory of blossoming.

YOUTH

Your youth is likely to be a difficult time. Most Pigs are misunderstood, even mocked, and you probably find this hard to bear. However, you do not strike out blindly, and neither do you seek revenge. Instead, you hold the pain close to your heart and carry on with your life.

FRIENDSHIPS

You may have difficulties in your friendships with people of your own age. This is because you naturally gravitate toward older people. You enjoy their wisdom, and they recognize your true personality. It is likely that these older people will become your very good friends.

They should provide you with valuable advice, as well as the necessary space to be yourself.

People of your own age group might consider you to be alienating, for you can sometimes appear to be overly self-possessed. It might occasionally prove beneficial to keep quiet and to let others speak, even if you consider their words to be silly. Try to resist the temptation to interrupt with your invariably good, but ultimately alienating, advice.

RELATIONSHIPS

You have the potential to enjoy a good emotional life. It is likely that your partner will appreciate you, and your committed relationship should be very happy.

PARENTHOOD

Your family should give you great pleasure. However, try not to expect

Pig Passing By

your children to share your sense of self-possession. In your maturity you may become overbearing. Try to control this trait, and allow your children to make their own mistakes.

PROSPECTS

It may seem hard, particularly in your youth, but you will simply have to learn to cope with your life when it becomes problematic. Do not despair, however, for any difficulties will invariably disappear once other people start to appreciate your essential worth.

As you grow older, your innate intelligence and skills are likely to become increasingly developed, and you should eventually become highly respected and admired.

PIG PASSING THE MOUNTAIN

~ 1947 2007 ~

This Pig possesses great talent and self-assurance.
Unfortunately, it also has a quick temper, which might lead
it to unwise decisions and hasty actions.

You are associated with a bee's sting. This means that you can sometimes be too quick and "stinging" in your choice of words. Try to keep your tendency to make tactless comments under control, for your ill-chosen words could destroy a valuable friendship.

PERSONALITY

You are likely to be very clever and talented. By nature, you are not particularly graceful, but you have probably compensated for any personal deficiencies by developing your wit and intellect instead.

Although this is largely advantageous, you must use your skills carefully. It is unlikely that many people will be as quick, clever, or sharp as you.

Your skills could cause much resentment, so use them wisely. Remember that if you try to tolerate other people, you might even learn from them and could add maturity to your natural intellect.

Once you have managed to curb your sharp tongue and quick wit, other people should find your company much more enjoyable, and correspondingly, your life should become easier.

Sometimes you are likely to feel very vulnerable. Perhaps you cannot bear to be the butt of another's wit, laughter, or scorn. This vulnerability may encourage you to strike the first blow in a confrontation or debate.

Do your best to learn to control this sense of vulnerability. It can often be a strength, for it relates to your innate sensitivity, but it could also push you into hasty actions that you might later regret.

Try to give yourself sufficient time to make the right decisions, and do not allow yourself to be pushed in

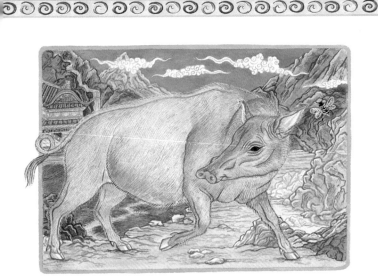

Pig Passing the Mountain

any way. Always remember your association with a bee sting – once the bee has stung, it dies.

CAREER

It is sometimes said that the Pig Passing the Mountain could live for very much longer, if it could only conserve its nervous energy. Perhaps you waste your valuable energy resources by trying too hard to be successful. Keep a careful watch on your stress levels, therefore, and make every conceivable effort to stay calm and relaxed.

RELATIONSHIPS

You are likely to have a good relationship with your partner, but it will have its stormy moments.

Try to take care in your relationships with your children. Unfortunately, you tend to expect rather too much from them, and consequently, rebellion might be their only possible response.

Give them the space to express themselves – even if you find it profoundly irritating to do so – and be prepared for this to improve your relationship considerably.

MONASTERY PIG

~ 1959 2019 ~

The ultimate threat to any Pig is being eaten. Chinese monks are vegetarian, however, and since this Pig lives in a monastery, it will never be threatened.

You are a very pampered Pig. You are associated with the warp and weft of thread, which hold together to make cloth. This association means that you have found a very secure, warm, and comfortable place for yourself.

PERSONALITY

Most Pigs are extremely bright and alert, and you are no exception. However, unlike many Pigs, you are not unduly frightened of being attacked or scorned by others. This innate sense of confidence and self-worth is likely to lead to a relaxed, comfortable life.

Fortune smiles on you, and you always seem to manage to be in the right place at the right time. It is unlikely, therefore, that you will ever experience any serious financial worries, and your life should be very good and enjoyable.

CAREER

You could be perceived as the classic self-made person. You have probably worked exceedingly hard to make your own destiny and have relied upon your renowned Pig wit, intelligence, and skill.

You tend to have a hearty dislike of anyone who uses deceit or cunning to make their way in the world. Your instinct is to move away from such people, or even to avoid them entirely.

However, at certain times you will probably have to challenge these people. Always try to handle these situations with care, and do not give in to the temptation of avoiding possible confrontation.

FRIENDSHIPS

It is a Pig characteristic to need only a few close friends. Even though you will gladly share your deepest

Monastery Pig

thoughts and feelings with these carefully chosen friends, other people might consider you to be distant and remote. However, the unflattering opinions of people who are not close to you will not bother you in the slightest.

RELATIONSHIPS

Once you have met your partner, you are likely to recognize virtually immediately that this is the person that you will be spending the rest of your life with.

PROSPECTS

As long as you remain true to yourself, you should be able to have a very good and content life. Because you manage to avoid many of life's normal anxieties, you are able to enjoy a certain sense of freedom. However, you should remember that you are particularly fortunate.

Do not allow your relative freedom from anxiety and worry to make you unsympathetic toward people who might have a more troubled life than your own.

PIG IN THE GARDEN

~ 1911 1971 ~

This is a very complex Pig. Its natural intelligence is combined with a certain brashness and lack of innate wisdom, which can lead to unnecessary trouble.

You are associated with punishment for committing an offense. This association can be perceived as a warning – do not overstep the mark.

Never mistake your intelligence for an intrinsic right to do as you please. When other people do not share your point of view, you might find that your cleverness is of little help. To avoid giving offense, try to control the use of your sharp wit.

PERSONALITY

You tend to be very self-possessed. This can be a good quality, as long as it does not tip you over into excessive conceit or disregard for other people. Sometimes you may try to avoid situations that are not directly useful to you. Although this can often be a sensible course of action, it can also mean that you are, or appear to be, cold and calculating. Learn to balance these aspects of

your personality, for it is very important that your self-possession does not turn into self-obsession.

YOUTH

Unfortunately, your early years at school and at work are likely to be rather frustrating and lonely. This is mainly because you are not particularly sociable, but also because your confidence and skills could make other people resentful.

This may result in spiteful and hurtful behavior toward you, and you could become increasingly lonely and introspective.

FRIENDSHIPS

Initially, it can prove difficult for you to make friends. This will invariably make your life problematic at times, but do not despair. As you grow older, you should make some very good, supportive friends.

Pig in the Garden

CAREER

It is likely that as other people mature, they will be able to accept, and even appreciate, your valuable qualities of self-possession and confidence. Consequently, your life should become easier, and you may even be able to accumulate some financial rewards.

PROSPECTS

Even though the beginning of your life will invariably be a troublesome time, you are still likely to rise to a respected position. You could become greatly honored, or even famous. Beware, for fame can be a lonely achievement, and remember that a balanced life is a happy life.

PIG IN THE FOREST

~ 1923 1983 ~

*This is a classic Pig. It leads a solitary life, it is obstinate,
yet it remains essentially fortunate. It does not worry about
the consequences of its actions.*

You are infinitely self-assured and tend to do whatever you want to do in life. You are likely to form extremely strong bonds with other people, and it usually takes a mighty blow for your opinion of them to change in any way.

PERSONALITY

You always prefer to rule your own life and wish to be free to do whatever you choose. Your sense of purpose and determination can rarely be questioned – once you have committed yourself to an idea or venture, virtually nothing will push you off course.

CAREER

It is likely to be difficult for you to fit yourself comfortably into any organization or structure. This is usually because you are brighter and more intelligent than those in authority, and consequently, you resent their impositions. You are therefore probably best suited to an individualistic, freelance existence.

It is very unlikely that you will ever be short of cash, so you should never feel insecure about financial matters. Relax and enjoy your money, for fortune will invariably shine on you.

FRIENDSHIPS

Your natural singlemindedness can be extremely admirable, but unfortunately, it does not always win you many friends.

Luckily, you have a well-developed streak of generosity. When you are confronted with real need you often act on impulse, and in times of great trouble, you will gladly support your friends or colleagues. Invariably, these altruistic actions are greatly appreciated.

Pig in the Forest

FAMILY

Unfortunately, you can occasionally be exasperating to others, and to your family in particular. Your long-suffering relatives may even consider you to be "pig-headed." Although this might seem to be an unfair accusation, you should try to show more generosity in your understanding of your family.

RELATIONSHIPS

In your emotional life, you are well advised to choose a partner who will always be your friend as well as your equal. Remember that you will only be able to love and respect someone with a personality at least as strong as your own.

A partner who is afraid of you, or who does not relish taking part in arguments, will always prove to be essentially unsuitable, and is therefore best avoided.

Occasionally, you may have to disagree very fiercely with your partner, but do not worry. As long as you chose your partner sensibly, you should be able to enjoy a very happy committed relationship.

Your Chinese Month of Birth

Find the table with your year of birth, and see where your birthday falls. For example, if you were born on August 30, 1959, you were born in Chinese month 7.

1 You are dogged in seeing things through, but can be rather slow. You should be successful in love.

2 You are a good friend. Do not give up when your life becomes difficult, for you should triumph.

3 You are full of bright ideas, but are unwilling to listen to others. Try to accept help and advice.

4 You are graceful and clever. Once you have overcome your shyness, you are good company.

5 You are nervous and dislike taking full responsibility. You much prefer to be in a supporting role.

6 You are quiet and seem to lack self-confidence. Be more positive, and seize your opportunities.

7 You are very fickle in your behavior. Beware, for you could destroy your potential happiness.

8 You are unlikely to have any serious worries. You are confident, capable, and should be successful.

9 You have abundant energy, but could become exhausted unless you learn to prioritize your projects.

10 You are very well balanced. You are open, capable, and always willing to listen to other people.

11 Your self-confidence can act as a barrier against others. You should be fortunate in business, however.

12 You are very sensitive. Always try to be positive, and be realistic in your assessment of situations.

* Some Chinese years contain double months:	
1911: Month 6	1947: Month 2
June 26 – July 25	Feb 21 – March 22
July 26 – Aug 23	March 23 – April 20
1971: Month 5	1995: Month 8
May 24 – June 22	Aug 26 – Sept 24
June 23 – July 21	Sept 25 – Oct 23

1911	
Jan 30 – Feb 28	1
March 1 – March 29	2
March 30 – April 28	3
April 29 – May 27	4
May 28 – June 25	5
* See double months box	6
Aug 24 – Sept 21	7
Sept 22 – Oct 21	8
Oct 22 – Nov 20	9
Nov 21 – Dec 19	10
Dec 20 – Jan 18 1912	11
Jan 19 – Feb 17	12

1923	
Feb 16 – March 16	1
March 17 – April 15	2
April 16 – May 15	3
May 16 – June 13	4
June 14 – July 13	5
July 14 – Aug 11	6
Aug 12 – Sept 10	7
Sept 11 – Oct 9	8
Oct 10 – Nov 7	9
Nov 8 – Dec 7	10
Dec 8 – Jan 5 1924	11
Jan 6 – Feb 4	12

1935	
Feb 4 – March 4	1
March 5 – April 2	2
April 3 – May 2	3
May 3 – May 31	4
June 1 – June 30	5
July 1 – July 29	6
July 30 – Aug 28	7
Aug 29 – Sept 27	8
Sept 28 – Oct 26	9
Oct 27 – Nov 25	10
Nov 26 – Dec 25	11
Dec 26 – Jan 23 1936	12

1947	
Jan 22 – Feb 20	1
* See double months box	2
April 21 – May 19	3
May 20 – June 18	4
June 19 – July 17	5
July 18 – Aug 15	6
Aug 16 – Sept 14	7
Sept 15 – Oct 13	8
Oct 14 – Nov 12	9
Nov 13 – Dec 11	10
Dec 12 – Jan 10 1948	11
Jan 11 – Feb 9	12

1959	
Feb 8 – March 8	1
March 9 – April 7	2
April 8 – May 7	3
May 8 – June 5	4
June 6 – July 5	5
July 6 – Aug 3	6
Aug 4 – Sept 2	7
Sept 3 – Oct 1	8
Oct 2 – Oct 31	9
Nov 1 – Nov 29	10
Nov 30 – Dec 29	11
Dec 30 – Jan 27 1960	12

1971	
Jan 27 – Feb 24	1
Feb 25 – March 26	2
March 27 – April 24	3
April 25 – May 23	4
* See double months box	5
July 22 – Aug 20	6
Aug 21 – Sept 18	7
Sept 19 – Oct 18	8
Oct 19 – Nov 17	9
Nov 18 – Dec 17	10
Dec 18 – Jan 15 1972	11
Jan 16 – Feb 14	12

1983	
Feb 13 – March 14	1
Mar 15 – April 12	2
April 13 – May 12	3
May 13 – June 10	4
June 11 – July 9	5
July 10 – Aug 8	6
Aug 9 – Sept 6	7
Sept 7 – Oct 5	8
Oct 6 – Nov 4	9
Nov 5 – Dec 3	10
Dec 4 – Jan 2 1984	11
Jan 3 – Feb 1	12

1995	
Jan 31 – Feb 28	1
Mar 1 – March 30	2
March 31 – April 29	3
April 30 – May 28	4
May 29 – June 27	5
June 28 – July 26	6
July 27 – July 25	7
* See double months box	8
Oct 24 – Nov 21	9
Nov 22 – Dec 21	10
Dec 22 – Jan 19 1996	11
Jan 20 – Feb 18	12

2007	
Feb 18 – March 18	1
March 19 – April 16	2
April 17 – May 16	3
May 17 – June 14	4
June 15 – July 13	5
July 14 – Aug 12	6
Aug 13 – Sept 10	7
Sept 11 – Oct 10	8
Oct 11 – Nov 9	9
Nov 10 – Dec 9	10
Dec 10 – Jan 7 2008	11
Jan 8 – Feb 6	12

YOUR CHINESE DAY OF BIRTH

Refer to the previous page to discover the beginning of your Chinese month of birth, then use the chart below to calculate your Chinese day of birth.

If you were born on May 5, 1911, your birthday is in the month starting on April 29. Find 29 on the chart below. Using 29 as the first day, count the days until you reach the date of your birthday. (Remember that not all months contain 31 days.) You were born on day 7 of the Chinese month.

If you were born in a Chinese double month, simply count the days from the first date of the month that contains your birthday.

1	2	3	4	5	6	7
8	9	10	11	12	13	14
15	16	17	18	19	20	21
22	23	24	25	26	27	28
29	30	31				

DAY 1, 10, 19, OR 28
You are trustworthy and set high standards, but tend to rush your

projects. Try to be cautious, and do not be too self-obsessed. You may receive unexpected money but must control your spending. You are suited to a career in the public sector or the arts.

DAY 2, 11, 20, OR 29
You are honest and popular. You need peace, but also require lively company. You are prone to outbursts of temper. You tend to enjoy life and make the most of your opportunities. You are suited to a literary or artistic career.

DAY 3, 12, 21, OR 30
You are quick-witted, but may appear to be difficult. As a result, people may be wary of being your friend. You have a disciplined character and fight for the truth. You are suited to careers that have a competitive element.

DAY 4, 13, 22, OR 31

You are very warmhearted, but also have a reserved attitude, which can sometimes make you appear unapproachable. If you try to be more outgoing and sociable, you should become more popular. You have a calm and patient manner, and are suited to a career as an academic or researcher.

DAY 5, 14, OR 23

Your fiery, obstinate nature can sometimes make it difficult for you to accept suggestions or opinions from others, and your stubbornness may lead to quarrels or problems. You should be lucky with money and may often use your profits to set up new projects. Your innate intelligence will enable you to cope with a demanding career.

DAY 6, 15, OR 24

You have an open, stable, and cheerful character, and enjoy an active social life. You are affectionate and emotional, and have a tendency to daydream. This can lead to confusion, and your eagerness to help others may be stifled by your indecision. Although you will never be wealthy, you should always have enough money.

DAY 7, 16, OR 25

You enjoy a certain amount of excitement in your life, but must learn to become more realistic and disciplined. Although you are a natural performer, you should beware of alienating your friends or colleagues. In your career, the opportunity to travel is more important to you than a good salary or a high standard of living.

DAY 8, 17, OR 26

You have very good judgment, but should not act too quickly. Your social skills may sometimes be lacking, and you may alienate other people, so try to be more tactful. You will experience poverty, but also wealth. Your calm and determined nature is combined with a free spirit, making you best suited to self-employment.

DAY 9, 18, OR 27

You are happy, optimistic, and warmhearted. You keep yourself busy and are rarely troubled by trivialities. Occasionally you quarrel unnecessarily with your friends, and it is important for you to learn to control your moods. You are particularly suited to a career as a sole owner or proprietor.

YOUR CHINESE
HOUR OF BIRTH

In Chinese time, one hour is equal to two Western hours.
Each Chinese double hour is associated with one of the
twelve astrological animals.

11 P.M. – 1 A.M. RAT HOUR
You are independent and have a hot temper. Try to think before you speak. Your thrifty nature will be useful in business and at home. You are willing to help those who are close to you, and they will return your support.

1 – 3 A.M. OX HOUR
Up to the age of twenty, your life could be difficult, but your fortunes are likely to improve after these troublesome years. In your career, be prepared to take a risk or to leave home during your youth to achieve your goals. You should enjoy a prosperous old age.

3 – 5 A.M. TIGER HOUR
You have a lively and creative nature, which may cause family arguments in your youth. Between the ages of twenty and forty you may have many problems. Luckily, your fortunes are likely to improve dramatically in your forties.

5 – 7 A.M. RABBIT HOUR
Your parents should be helpful, but your siblings may be your rivals. You may have to move away from home to achieve your full potential at work. Your committed relationship may take time to become settled, but you should get along much better with everyone after middle age.

7 – 9 A.M. DRAGON HOUR
You have a quick-witted, determined, and attractive nature. Your life will be busy, but you could sometimes be lonely. You should achieve a good standard of living. Try to curb your excessive self-confidence, for it could make working relationships difficult.

9 – 11 A.M. SNAKE HOUR
You have a talent for business and should find it easy to build your career and provide for your family. You have a very generous spirit and will gladly help your friends when they are in trouble. Unfortunately, family relationships are unlikely to run smoothly.

11 A.M. – 1 P.M. HORSE HOUR
You are active, clever, and obstinate. Try to listen to advice. You are fascinated with travel and with changing your life. Learn to control your extravagance, for it could lead to financial suffering.

1 – 3 P.M. RAM HOUR
Steady relationships with your family, friends, or partners are difficult, because you have an active nature. You are clever, but must not force your views on others. Your fortunes will be at their lowest in your middle age.

3 – 5 P.M. MONKEY HOUR
You earn and spend money easily. Your character is attractive, but frustrating, too. Sometimes your parents are not able to give you adequate moral support. Your committed relationship should be good, but do not brood over emotional problems for too long – if you do your career could suffer.

5 – 7 P.M. ROOSTER HOUR
In your teenage years you may have many arguments with your family. There could even be a family division, which should eventually be resolved. You are trustworthy, kind, and warmhearted, and never intend to hurt other people.

7 – 9 P.M. DOG HOUR
Your brave, capable, hard-working nature is ideally suited to self-employment, and the forecast for your career is excellent. Try to control your impatience and vanity. The quality of your life is far more important to you than the amount of money you have saved.

9 – 11 P.M. PIG HOUR
You are particularly skilled at manual work and always set yourself high standards. Although you are warmhearted, you do not like to surround yourself with too many friends. However, the people who are close to you have your complete trust. You can be easily upset by others, but are able to forgive and forget quickly.

YOUR FORTUNE IN OTHER ANIMAL YEARS

The Pig's fortunes fluctuate during the twelve animal years.
It is best to concentrate on a year's positive aspects, and to
take care when faced with the seemingly negative.

YEAR OF THE RAT

Although troubles in your professional life may seem to loom constantly, the Pig is fortunate in the Year of the Rat. Consequently you should find that these problems fade away, without any great effort being necessary on your part.

YEAR OF THE OX

You are likely to enjoy an excellent social life during the Year of the Ox. Unfortunately, this frenetic activity could prove to be a serious drain on your financial resources, as well as a cause of considerable friction for other people.

YEAR OF THE TIGER

To start with, it may seem as if the Year of the Tiger is a natural continuation of last year's social excesses. The main difference this year, however, is that you have learned to save as well as to spend.

YEAR OF THE RABBIT

Your social life and your professional life are highly auspicious in the Year of the Rabbit, and you should enjoy considerable success in every area of your life. Other people will stay close to your side, in the hope that your success is contagious.

YEAR OF THE DRAGON

Previously undiscovered leadership qualities will reveal themselves to you in the Year of the Dragon. These are extremely precious talents, and they should be developed fully, for they will enable you to exert much more control over your life.

YEAR OF THE SNAKE

This is a year of mixed fortunes. You will enjoy success, but you will experience failure, too. The start of the year should be your most successful period. After this time, you will fritter away your financial rewards on trivialities.

YEAR OF THE HORSE

You are likely to be annoyed with yourself this year for not making the most of last year's opportunities. Regretting the past is a waste of effort, however, and your energy would be better spent in enduring this very difficult year.

YEAR OF THE RAM

In your professional life you should be successful and are likely to gain some form of promotion. Do not get carried away by this success, however, because the Year of the Ram could also make you suffer some personal misfortunes.

YEAR OF THE MONKEY

Although financial affairs are auspicious in the Year of the Monkey, you should remember that although money is useful, it does not necessarily bring happiness. If you learn to use your wealth wisely, you will achieve the most benefits.

YEAR OF THE ROOSTER

All your hard work may seem to be fruitless during the Year of the Rooster. Try not to become dispirited or impatient, because this will detract from your diligent efforts. Keep calm and your life can only improve.

YEAR OF THE DOG

This is a very odd year, in which nothing seems to work out in quite the way that you had expected. Luckily, the strange events experienced during the Year of the Dog should not have a detrimental effect on your long-term happiness.

YEAR OF THE PIG

It would be unwise to make many plans in the Year of the Pig, or to hold too many hopes. It is a year of great instability; therefore, it would be most beneficial if you keep a low profile and look forward to better times.

YOUR CHINESE YEAR OF BIRTH

Your astrological animal corresponds to the Chinese year of your birth. It is the single most important key in the quest to unlock your Chinese horoscope.

Find your Western year of birth in the left-hand column of the chart. Your Chinese astrological animal is on the same line as your year of birth in the right-hand column of the chart. If you were born in the beginning of the year, check the middle column of the chart carefully. For example, if you were born in 1972, you might assume that you belong to the Year of the Rat. However, if your birthday falls before February 15, you actually belong to the Year of the Pig.

1900	Jan 31 – Feb 18, 1901	Rat	1917	Jan 23 – Feb 10, 1918	Snake
1901	Feb 19 – Feb 7, 1902	Ox	1918	Feb 11 – Jan 31, 1919	Horse
1902	Feb 8 – Jan 28, 1903	Tiger	1919	Feb 1 – Feb 19, 1920	Ram
1903	Jan 29 – Feb 15, 1904	Rabbit	1920	Feb 20 – Feb 7, 1921	Monkey
1904	Feb 16 – Feb 3, 1905	Dragon	1921	Feb 8 – Jan 27, 1922	Rooster
1905	Feb 4 – Jan 24, 1906	Snake	1922	Jan 28 – Feb 15, 1923	Dog
1906	Jan 25 – Feb 12, 1907	Horse	1923	Feb 16 – Feb 4, 1924	Pig
1907	Feb 13 – Feb 1, 1908	Ram	1924	Feb 5 – Jan 23, 1925	Rat
1908	Feb 2 – Jan 21, 1909	Monkey	1925	Jan 24 – Feb 12, 1926	Ox
1909	Jan 22 – Feb 9, 1910	Rooster	1926	Feb 13 – Feb 1, 1927	Tiger
1910	Feb 10 – Jan 29, 1911	Dog	1927	Feb 2 – Jan 22, 1928	Rabbit
1911	Jan 30 – Feb 17, 1912	Pig	1928	Jan 23 – Feb 9, 1929	Dragon
1912	Feb 18 – Feb 5, 1913	Rat	1929	Feb 10 – Jan 29, 1930	Snake
1913	Feb 6 – Jan 25, 1914	Ox	1930	Jan 30 – Feb 16, 1931	Horse
1914	Jan 26 – Feb 13, 1915	Tiger	1931	Feb 17 – Feb 5, 1932	Ram
1915	Feb 14 – Feb 2, 1916	Rabbit	1932	Feb 6 – Jan 25, 1933	Monkey
1916	Feb 3 – Jan 22, 1917	Dragon	1933	Jan 26 – Feb 13, 1934	Rooster

1934	Feb 14 – Feb 3, 1935	Dog		1971	Jan 27 – Feb 14, 1972	Pig
1935	Feb 4 – Jan 23, 1936	Pig		1972	Feb 15 – Feb 2, 1973	Rat
1936	Jan 24 – Feb 10, 1937	Rat		1973	Feb 3 – Jan 22, 1974	Ox
1937	Feb 11 – Jan 30, 1938	Ox		1974	Jan 23 – Feb 10, 1975	Tiger
1938	Jan 31 – Feb 18, 1939	Tiger		1975	Feb 11 – Jan 30, 1976	Rabbit
1939	Feb 19 – Feb 7, 1940	Rabbit		1976	Jan 31 – Feb 17, 1977	Dragon
1940	Feb 8 – Jan 26, 1941	Dragon		1977	Feb 18 – Feb 6, 1978	Snake
1941	Jan 27 – Feb 14, 1942	Snake		1978	Feb 7 – Jan 27, 1979	Horse
1942	Feb 15 – Feb 4, 1943	Horse		1979	Jan 28 – Feb 15, 1980	Ram
1943	Feb 5 – Jan 24, 1944	Ram		1980	Feb 16 – Feb 4, 1981	Monkey
1944	Jan 25 – Feb 12, 1945	Monkey		1981	Feb 5 – Jan 24, 1982	Rooster
1945	Feb 13 – Feb 1, 1946	Rooster		1982	Jan 25 – Feb 12, 1983	Dog
1946	Feb 2 – Jan 21, 1947	Dog		1983	Feb 13 – Feb 1, 1984	Pig
1947	Jan 22 – Feb 9, 1948	Pig		1984	Feb 2 – Feb 19, 1985	Rat
1948	Feb 10 – Jan 28, 1949	Rat		1985	Feb 20 – Feb 8, 1986	Ox
1949	Jan 29 – Feb 16, 1950	Ox		1986	Feb 9 – Jan 28, 1987	Tiger
1950	Feb 17 – Feb 5, 1951	Tiger		1987	Jan 29 – Feb 16, 1988	Rabbit
1951	Feb 6 – Jan 26, 1952	Rabbit		1988	Feb 17 – Feb 5, 1989	Dragon
1952	Jan 27 – Feb 13, 1953	Dragon		1989	Feb 6 – Jan 26, 1990	Snake
1953	Feb 14 – Feb 2, 1954	Snake		1990	Jan 27 – Feb 14, 1991	Horse
1954	Feb 3 – Jan 23, 1955	Horse		1991	Feb 15 – Feb 3, 1992	Ram
1955	Jan 24 – Feb 11, 1956	Ram		1992	Feb 4 – Jan 22, 1993	Monkey
1956	Feb 12 – Jan 30, 1957	Monkey		1993	Jan 23 – Feb 9, 1994	Rooster
1957	Jan 31 – Feb 17, 1958	Rooster		1994	Feb 10 – Jan 30, 1995	Dog
1958	Feb 18 – Feb 7, 1959	Dog		1995	Jan 31 – Feb 18, 1996	Pig
1959	Feb 8 – Jan 27, 1960	Pig		1996	Feb 19 – Feb 6, 1997	Rat
1960	Jan 28 – Feb 14, 1961	Rat		1997	Feb 7 – Jan 27, 1998	Ox
1961	Feb 15 – Feb 4, 1962	Ox		1998	Jan 28 – Feb 15, 1999	Tiger
1962	Feb 5 – Jan 24, 1963	Tiger		1999	Feb 16 – Feb 4, 2000	Rabbit
1963	Jan 25 – Feb 12, 1964	Rabbit		2000	Feb 5 – Jan 23, 2001	Dragon
1964	Feb 13 – Feb 1, 1965	Dragon		2001	Jan 24 – Feb 11, 2002	Snake
1965	Feb 2 – Jan 20, 1966	Snake		2002	Feb 12 – Jan 31, 2003	Horse
1966	Jan 21 – Feb 8, 1967	Horse		2003	Feb 1 – Jan 21, 2004	Ram
1967	Feb 9 – Jan 29, 1968	Ram		2004	Jan 22 – Feb 8, 2005	Monkey
1968	Jan 30 – Feb 16, 1969	Monkey		2005	Feb 9 – Jan 28, 2006	Rooster
1969	Feb 17 – Feb 5, 1970	Rooster		2006	Jan 29 – Feb 17, 2007	Dog
1970	Feb 6 – Jan 26, 1971	Dog		2007	Feb 18 – Feb 6, 2008	Pig

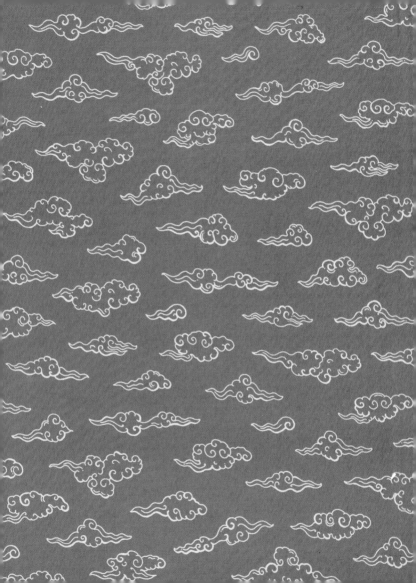